SAVE
The DAY

LEARNING TO EMBRACE YOUR INNER HERO

MAURICE F. MARTIN

PUBLISHING

Courageous Faith Publishing

Save the Day

Copyright © 2021 Maurice F. MartinRequests for information should be addressed to:Courageous Faith Publishing, 1225 Packard Dr. Akron, Ohio 44320

ISBN 978-0-578-30229-4

Cover design by Michael Chase

Hero Author Graphic by Marleena Jones

First printing, 2021.

Printed in the United States of America

Dedication

Ashleigh and Naima Martin, thank you for being my greatest inspiration and proof of God's love and grace in my life.

Calvin (Pop) and Cynthia Ridley (Mom), thank you for believing in me and for the role you've played in helping my writing come to life.

Mary Jean Fleming, thank you for helping me to find my superpowers and for holding me up when I wasn't strong enough to stand on my own.

Waymer Martin, for unconditional love and immovable support, I am forever thankful. You are a true gift from God to the World, and I wouldn't be where I am if it wasn't for you.

Curtis and Ann Snipes, thank you for all of your prayers, your words of wisdom, and your unwavering support.

Maria Bonner, thank you for your mentorship and your prayers. Thank you for the transparency and vulnerability that you extend as you go after everything that God has for you. It is an inspiration and an honor to walk with you.

Jeff Gargas, thank you for your consistent mentorship, support, and unshakeable belief. I wouldn't be who I am today if I had never met you. I appreciate you more than you know.

Michael Chase, thank you for blessing this book with your time and talent. I am honored and humbled to have worked with you.

Casey Novak, thank you for taking the time and energy to help this book shine. You have always been a true friend and for that I am forever grateful.

Dennis Castiglione, thank you for the time and attention that you paid to this book. You jumped in and pushed the book to another level simply because of the man you are. You are changing so many lives and I continue to be so proud of you!

Erwin Martin Jr., you'll never get to read these words, but please know that you've been the wind beneath my wings and will forever be a driving force in my life. When I fly, we fly together little brother. I love you.

Contents

Foreword

"I think a hero is an ordinary individual who finds strength to persevere and endure in spite of overwhelming obstacles. "

-Christopher Reeve

The size of this book is no indication of the magnitude of wisdom and practicality that it contains.

I am fortunate and honored to have had God connect my journey to the life and journey of Maurice F Martin! Witnessing the faith, courage, trust, and purity of his walk has been inspiring & life giving. Maurice has poured himself into the pages of this book and I pray that as I did, you also will gain wisdom and encouragement "...to view who you are with a lens of accuracy and honesty."

Maurice offers us a different perspective that opposes mainstream's idea of self-help! His vulnerability, transparency, and life experiences are gracefully used to give us a framework to "Begin to discover or rediscover who you are."

As you read through the pages of this book you will be

challenged to be 'intentional and introspective'. You will be invited to identify your kryptonite; in hope that you "eliminate those things that are killing you."

Maurice's written words resonate with inspiration, motivation, encouragement, and practicality. Inspired and motivated, by understanding that "Becoming great is not about building your ego...that life is about grace, not status... Becoming great has nothing to do with titles, dollars in a bank account, or perceptions of society. This is about you becoming the greatest version of yourself, so the lives standing in front of you, and the lives of those fortunate enough to be around you are better because you lived." You will be encouraged by knowing that you are not alone in this journey called life! Encouraged by knowing that there are others with similar experiences who have endured hardships and yet have tasted progressive victories! Encouraged by being reminded that "You've been empowered by Power and loved by Love."

Lastly, you aren't just given encouragement, but Maurice was intentional to equip us with practical and pragmatic tools to begin and sustain the journey towards health and healing!

-Maria Bonner, LPC, MACC

Servant Leader | The Gathering Space

Introduction

What's wrong with you? What's right with you? What do you need more of in your life? What do you need to flat out quit? These questions are pivotal for any person who is looking to heal, grow, and mature in life. Your answers may set the course of your future.

If you seek to become a more whole and healthier individual, you will need to act with a mindset of intentionality. Intention is at the heart of personal growth - intentionally get better or stay stuck where you are. We all experience times where we wish life was like the movies. If only someone could fly in and rescue us from the lowest and most dangerous moments of our lives.

Unfortunately, life is not a superhero film and no one is flying in to save you. Whether this book is reaching you during a bad month, a rough year, or a difficult decade, it is imperative for you to understand that the hero you are waiting for is the person staring back at you in the mirror. You are the one who will need to think and live with a sense of intentionality, wisdom, faith, and courage.

Improving your life must begin with a high level of introspection. Who are you today? If you haven't been functioning at your highest capacity, what are the things you can do right now to start moving in the right direction? Once you establish that, you must decide what must die in your life so you can live the life you dream of.

Now, that probably sounds overly dramatic but let me ask you a few questions. Is anything secretly killing a part of you? Are elements of your daily life destroying your passion, your optimism, or your hope? What kryptonite is draining you of the strength and ability to fight back?

The reality is, if you're going to take your life back, you must eliminate these things that are killing you. You're strong enough. You're valuable enough. You're worthy of a better life. That is not all, someone is praying for you. I'm not talking about your prayer circle or your personal prayer warriors. Instead, I am here to remind you that living your best life is the answer to someone else's prayer.

To live a life empowered and with purpose is necessary for you and those who love you. This includes those you were born to impact, although you may not have met them yet. I realize that it can be hard to imagine being empowered today if you are feeling lost.

I remember a time in my life when I was living a life that was less than my best. From the outside, I seemed happy and successful. As an up-and-coming singer in the music industry, my band had success. I won awards as a singer and signed national deals as a songwriter. From studio sessions with Grammy winners to music videos with Emmy winners, it looked like my life had the makings of a beautiful story.

Behind the scenes, my life was anything but beautiful. I was broken, depressed, and empty. No accomplishment gave me peace. No words of praise that rained into my life made up for the tears that rained down my face when I was alone. No applause could fill the void. I felt alone.

The deeper into the darkness I sank, the more helpless I felt. I tried to fill the void with work, drinking, sex, food, and so many other things. Nothing helped. Nothing outside of me could fix what was broken on the inside. I felt out of sync, out of purpose, and out of touch with life.

"Was I born to always be miserable?"

"Is change really possible for me?"

"'Am I too broken to get better?"

"Is there really a point to moving forward in my life?

Maybe you've been asking many of the same questions. I want to begin this book by letting you know that it is not too late for you to change your life. That sentiment is the driving force behind the work that I do. The change that you're searching for can begin today.

I know. You may feel like you are a lost cause. I remember feeling that way too. You may have a look of hopelessness and helplessness in your eyes that I have seen in so many clients that I've worked with.

I was not helpless. They were not helpless. You are not helpless. My primary objective in writing this book was to be a messenger of hope for people who are feeling hopeless. I believe that you can get better, and my prayer is that you will begin to see that for yourself.

The key to transformation is found within you. You can connect to the purpose that God has put you on the earth to fulfill. In the end, my redemption became the fulfillment of someone else's prayer. Someone is praying for you to get through this in the same way.

In this book, I will share with you five concepts to challenge your perspective. Hopefully, they will provide a spark if your flame is not burning as brightly as possible. I didn't write this book to prove to you how smart I am or how great of a speaker and coach I am. I wrote this book to let you know that change starts now, and it starts in you.

Reflections

Chapter 1

Walk

TOWARDS IT

"You can wreck your future running from your past." This powerful statement by Bishop TD Jakes has rang true for seasons of my life; seasons when all my attention and energy became transfixed on my past. Guilt. Shame. Remorse. Regret. All the woulda, coulda, and shoulda moments left me less than my best and not present in the moment.

Are you at a similar place in your life? It's nothing to be ashamed of. However, this is something you need to end to make the absolute most of this moment. For many of you, perhaps things seem a bit foggy as of late. Time appears to be flying by, yet it seems you are moving in slow motion or worse, frozen in time.

If this describes you, I want you to know there is hope for you. As a counselor and life coach, countless individuals I've worked with, felt as though they were stuck in their minds. Life can sometimes feel like running a marathon in a hamster wheel; all of the tiring mileage without seeing progress. Getting lost in your past tends to bring depression; racing into your future brings anxiety. Neither are fun or easy things to deal with, but the solution to both issues is to live your life in the "here and now". You can't change the past but you can heal and grow from your past now.

You can't control the future, but you can work today to become healthier for when the future arrives. Fixing your life involves making the most of each precious day. Your power comes from this moment; it requires you to be fully mindful, present, and aware of the moment you are in.

For many of us, fears about the future are born from issues we have been running from in our past. These issues include childhood wounds, heartbreaks, disappointment, and consequences from bad decisions. We run from what we've been through, hoping we can reach a safe space. Sadly, many of us never find the safety we desire. We hope accomplishments, new relationships, or substances can provide us with the relief we desire. Nevertheless, all these things can leave us empty and void of the transformations we seek. If my words resonate a bit too much with you, I need to tell you something. Now is the time for you to stop running from your shadow.

We all are aware of the calling card of a superhero; they run into danger to save the day. However, in our daily lives, we often find ourselves cowering in fear while longing to stand tall. I often say people run from what God is calling them to walk towards. In scripture, the Disciple Peter advises, "Consider it pure joy, my brothers and sisters, whenever you face trials of many kinds because you know that the testing of your faith produces perseverance. Let perseverance finish its work so that you may be mature and complete, not lacking anything." (James 1:2-4).

The moments in life that test your faith or the challenges placed in front of you, help you grow and become whoever God is calling you to become. Regrettably, many of us hit those tests and trials but consider them anything but pure joy. We consider them hell and run, crying and screaming. We are left as a fraction of who we used to be instead of using the difficulty to mature and grow.

As you move forward, you must decide if you will continue to run from these moments. Will you let those moments that haunted you begin to help you mature and grow? This growth can be the key to unlocking the version of you, God is calling you to become.

Dealing with pain can be difficult, but aren't you already hurting? You need to decide whether you will continue to stay locked in a mental prison or do the work that will allow you to heal from those moments. At some point in your mental prison, your inner critic becomes your greatest nemesis. The negativity, insults, doubts and trauma cloud your perception and pain can skew your perspective.

Whether you choose therapy, grief counseling, rehab, or fasting and prayer, something must

partner with your faith to increase your mental clarity and emotional health. If faith without works is dead (James 2:17), obedience to the strategy and plan of God brings life. If you are praying for God to deliver you, remember that miracles, signs, wonders, and deliverance flow out of proper positioning. Your positioning is the result of partnership with the Holy Spirit. If nothing is changing in your situation, something needs to change in your actions. Understand, you don't need to be a victim of circumstance. You have a say in what you do with this pain. You can do the work required to break through this pain or the pain will continue to break you. This is not a simple task, but as we realize, not many things in life are simple. Life is complicated and so is healing. Yet, the start of the healing process is rather simple. Be intentional about doing the work, starting today. When tomorrow comes, you will be living today again; so keep doing the work today. Try different methods, leave no stone unturned until you find health and healing.

I know. You are haunted by parts of your past. A creature seems to be lurking behind you, waiting to attack the moment you find a sense of peace or joy. For many years, you've been running to escape your shadow. Here is the good news. If a giant shadow is behind you, remember there must be a source of light ahead of you. Your brightest days are ahead of you! If you can perceive your shadow, believe God can use it.

The you
of *today*
is the *shadow*
of the you
of your *destiny.*

"As a result, people brought the sick into the streets and laid them on beds and mats so that at least Peter's shadow might fall on some of them as he passed by. Crowds gathered also from the towns around Jerusalem, bringing their sick and those tormented by impure spirits, and all of them were healed." (Acts 5:15-16).

Like Peter's shadow healed people on the streets, someone can be healed by yours. The testimony of what God has brought you through can be the very thing someone else needs the most in their life. This may provide them with the faith and hope they also need to heal. The you of today is the shadow of the you of your destiny. Heal today so a future version of you can be used by God in a mighty way. A way beyond your comprehension.

Getting better isn't only for you. Healing today begins the formation of your testimony. Your testimony will bring healing to someone who is saying a prayer today. Your health and healing are integral to their answered prayer. You matter. You are important. Stop running from your shadow. Walk towards your brokenness and dysfunction and let God use what once broke you to build you. What the enemy meant for evil, God will use for your good! (Genesis 50:20) Believe this, if God is for you, nothing can stand against you!

Reflections

Chapter 2

Greatness

WITHIN

What is your greatest fear? I'll give you a moment to think.

Got it? Next question. What fear is holding you back the most? I'll give some more time.

Now, the most important question. Are those two fears the same? When asked about a person's greatest fear, people tend to think of things such as snakes, dogs, the dark, failure, or dying alone. When you are asked what fear is holding you back, the answer is often completely different.

If you're being *honest,* many of you fear *being great.*

If you're being honest, many of you fear...being great. You are afraid to accomplish the things you deeply desire in your life.

You might say to yourself "What if success is too much for me to handle?"

"Would I get caught up in the attention?"

"Will my family be able to handle my transformation?"

"Can I put in the work to build a legacy?"

"I've screwed up some things in my past, if I fail again, I can't live it down!

I want to encourage you today. If you are someone who has a deep-down fear of your greatness, it's time to embrace the plan God has for you. Regardless of what your past looks like, if you're still on planet Earth, you are here for a reason. Whether it's the book you're meant to write, the love you need to pour into your children, or the amazing roads that you need to build in your city, I want to challenge you to be the very best you can be.

It is a *humbling* process of tearing down the *limiting beliefs* that we believe about ourselves and embracing the *possibilities* of what God can do in and *through* us.

Dr. Martin Luther King Jr. once said, "If a man is called to be a street sweeper, he should sweep streets even as Michelangelo painted, or Beethoven composed music or Shakespeare wrote poetry. He should sweep streets so well that all the hosts of heaven and earth will pause to say, here lived a great street sweeper who did his job well."

We can acknowledge that greatness is a relative term, but there are ways to measure if you're as great as you could be. One way to measure greatness is to ask yourself if you are afraid to do the work that is required to be the best you can be. Many men are willing to go through years of schooling to become amazing architects who can build beautiful structures. However, those same men refuse to go to marital counseling to build a powerful marriage. Some women work tirelessly to build up their husbands and children. They, too, refuse to do the work to build their self-esteem. I challenge you today to fix those areas of your life where you are scared of becoming healthy and whole. Be the incredible father you wanted and needed. Become the attentive teacher you wished led your classroom. Evolve into a business owner who builds up, rather than tears-down their employees.

Becoming great is not about building your ego. Instead, it is a humbling process of tearing down the "limiting beliefs" that we believe about ourselves and embracing the possibilities of what God can do in and through us.

If you are anything like me, you are learning that life is about grace, not status. The most beautiful moments in life are priceless moments you don't need to earn. Jesus paid a price for you and some opportunities are afforded to you simply because of His love. Now, you have a chance to walk in God's abundance and greatness. Becoming great has nothing to do with titles, dollars in a bank account, or our perceptions of society. This is about you becoming the greatest version of yourself, so the lives standing in front of you, and the lives of those fortunate enough to be around you are better just because you have lived. You may have started moving down that path. If you've lost momentum and become stagnant, today is a good day to stop running from your greatness and begin walking towards the change someone around you needs.

Reflections

Chapter 3

Quit

NEGLECTING WHAT YOU NEED

Repeat after me, "It isn't ok."

Say it out loud, "It isn't ok."

If you haven't said it, I hope by the end of this chapter, you will say it out of principle.

Beloved, don't continue to neglect what you need for the wants of others. You matter. Your health and well-being matters, as well. Sometimes we want so badly to take care of others that we forget to look after ourselves. This doesn't work and never will.

You have such a *beautiful* heart. You sincerely want what is best for others. The problem is you don't apply the same *love, attention,* or *affection* to yourself.

In the last chapter, I used words like health and healing repeatedly. Now we need to take a moment to get honest. If you are unhealthy in your mind, body, or soul, you are likely polluting the very people you're trying to love. I understand those words may sound harsh. However, when you have dealt with some of the things you've lived through, a lasting impression is left. That which has cut you deeply can lead to you bleeding on others if you have not fully healed.

Do you ever find yourself feeling overwhelmingly emotional, frustrated, or short-tempered, even when you're trying to do right by others? Are you tired and lethargic in your daily life? If you're running on "E", working on strengthening your mind, body, and spirit is not merely something nice to want. It's what you need.

You have such a beautiful heart. You sincerely want what is best for others. The problem is you don't apply the same love, attention, or affection to yourself. Moreover, you may not have set up healthy boundaries with loved ones. Loved ones can suck out all your positive energy. You pour into them but truthfully, they pour nothing back. Now here you are, a lifeless version of the person you expect to be. When people ask how you are, it's always the same answer, "I'm ok," or "I'm fine."

You are not fine and you are justified to say so.

In John 10:10, Jesus explains, "The thief comes only to steal, kill, and destroy. I came that they may have life and have it abundantly." If you are a believer and you are feeling empty, we need to talk. You are not supposed to feel this low. If you are feeling a lack of joy, happiness, or peace, something is wrong. Many of us have experienced life void of God's abundance for far too long. If you have been convinced that this is "normal", you have been convinced of a lie.

The emptiness that you feel is not ok. Even if you are mourning or hurting from a painful situation, scripture promises peace that surpasses all understanding (Philippians 4:7 ESV). There's enough peace available that you can be filled up and your loved ones can be affected by your overflow. There's enough joy for you to be filled up and leave those around you touched by what radiates from you. An abundant life is available for you, but you have to stop neglecting your needs. Instead, take back what is rightfully yours and walk in the fullness of what is possible. Walk in the fullness of God.

Whatever or whoever convinced you that it was ok to always sacrifice your happiness, did you a disservice.

If you are clinging to those beliefs instead of doing the work to become healthy, whole, or at peace with your life, you are doing yourself a disservice. I want to challenge you to sit down with a pencil and a pad tonight and ask yourself, "What do I need in my life?" Be honest with yourself! There are segments of your life that are bone dry, but as He did with the Prophet Ezekiel (Ezekiel 37:1-14), God is calling you to speak life into the dead spaces of your existence.

Speak hope. Speak positively about what your future can become. Stop believing you are always supposed to be empty and alone. It isn't right and isn't true. There is a beautiful world out there for the taking, but that life is reached by honestly seeking out what areas of your life are broken and need to be fixed. I will remind you again, the one to fly in and save the day is you! Yes, it can be hard work to mend, repair, and rebuild what has been broken in you, but the work will be worth it in the end. How you feel today isn't ok. Acknowledging that, is the start of being empowered to do something about it.

Reflections

_____
_____
_____
_____
_____
_____
_____
_____
_____
_____
_____
_____
_____
_____
_____
_____
_____
_____
_____
_____
_____
_____
_____
_____
_____
_____
_____
_____
_____
_____
_____

Chapter 4

You

ARE ENOUGH

I won't try to make you repeat after me, but I do want to plant a seed in your spirit that you are enough. You're enough to hope for and believe in. You're valuable enough to be invested in with time, love, and healthy attention. You're enough for all of it, but if you're not able to discern it, you may be living a life less fulfilling than the one possible for you.

One of the confusing things about the human experience is that most humans base concepts like self-worth and self-esteem on the feedback and opinions of others. Things that are meant to be perceived and nurtured from within tend to become an outside-in process. In other words, I should form belief systems and values inwardly which are confirmed by the world. In an inside-out process, I learn that I'm a good person, then people who get to know me are able to confirm what I understand about myself. In that system of thinking and living, a person who approaches me and believes something untrue will automatically trigger a red flag internally. I believe I'm a good person. I have not done anything wrong to the person, he or she has a questionable character and is projecting his or her feelings and thoughts onto me. I can identify it, move from it and be stronger because of it. That is how interactions should take place in life. Sadly though, many people miss out on this enlightened way of living.

Instead, many individuals take 100% of the perception of their identity from outside sources.

Whatever Mom said about me is true. Whatever the haters called me is the identity I'll take on. My understanding of me is less important than their perception of me, even if they barely know me.

If you're surrounded by a loving community of individuals who invest in getting to know you intimately, perhaps this system can lead to a healthy understanding of who you are. Certainly, this can solidify the building of healthy self-esteem.

Some of you who are reading this book are fortunate. People who loved you always held a mirror in front of you and helped you see both who you were and who you could be. If you are in that category, I'm happy for you and I pray you are paying that forward to your loved ones.

However, if those who helped form your identity failed to speak life into you, you must change how you perceive yourself. This is possible even if you've spent a lifetime being filled with lies and misconceptions about your true identity.

Now before I move forward, I want to make sure

I am crystal clear that none of us should live on an emotional island where all thoughts and opinions of others are irrelevant. People around us provide additional clarity, perspective, and awareness. These are critical services, but should be secondary.

Many of us wear a mask that hides us from the world. If you don't comprehend how incredible the person underneath your mask is, there is a problem. You must view who you are with a lens of accuracy and honesty. The journey to a better life begins with you opening your eyes and examining your own life.

What are you good at? What are your superpowers? What are the areas of your life worth pouring time, love, and resources into? Scripture says that you have been "fearfully and wonderfully made" by God! (Psalm 139:14). It is imperative that you get to know the person God envisioned you to be. You must do the work to find those things. Exercises like prayer, journaling, and free writing can be integral to learning who you are.

Failure to **heal** will leave you looking at **life** through a *skewed* and *confused* lens.

Begin to discover or rediscover who you are. Only then, can you begin to take in the feedback with the ability to perceive and believe what people say. Let's face it: when we develop our self-image, self-worth, and self-esteem from the outside, most of our minds cling to the negative feedback we receive. Fifty men can tell you that you are beautiful but if you don't know and recognize your own beauty, it only takes one telling you that you're ugly for you to believe you are. It is crazy but true for so many.

I want to challenge and charge you today to begin doing the difficult work to identify who you are. What people observe is less important than what you learn about yourself.

If you aren't yet doing work to be mentally and spiritually healthy and to grow through grief, pain, traumas, or tragedies, then this work is critical for you. Failure to heal will leave you looking at life through a skewed and confused lens.

You may notice the repeated trends in this book of health and healing. I want to reiterate that what is broken in you will seep out of you, leaving you less than your best self. It will also leave you vulnerable to people who use your lack of self-confidence to their advantage. There are corporations and suitors alike who prey on you, neglecting your worth. Whether it affects you emotionally, financially, or physically, it has to stop. The only one who can stop it is you!

If learning about yourself reveals areas of your life where you are in a place of lack, you have identified the areas where you need to start doing the work. Build up those areas. If you lack knowledge, sign up for classes and build your skills. If you need to be built up in your body, devote yourself to engaging in healthier eating habits and physical workout routines. If you need to be built up holistically, ask God to reveal to you how He sees you during your prayer time. Meditate on what scripture says about you. If you find areas where you don't see value or worth, those are the areas where you need to build yourself up. As scripture advises, "encourage yourself." (1 Samuel 30:6 KJV).

I often tell clients that the start of their day is the greatest time to practice self-care. Begin with something like a gratitude journal. What are you most grateful for today? It may help you to see how cherished you are by the power that is greater than you, things you've been carried through and delivered from because of God's grace. After gratitude, consider positive affirmations about yourself, write things that you believe or need to believe about your worth and value. Write down what scriptures say about you. Write down things that the Holy Spirit has said to you during prayer times.

These types of exercises tend to be practiced more by women than men. In my experience, men have an equal level of deficiency in their perceived value as women. They are often less aware of it or unable to acknowledge it, but the issues are there. If you are a man, I charge you to be honest with yourself. Analyze if you have a strong level of self-esteem, self-worth, and self-control in your life. If you don't, do the work.

This work isn't specific to gender; it is specific to those who need to learn and then walk in the purpose they were born to live. Whoever you are, I want you to know you are worth doing the work. You are enough, but it is not enough for me to affirm that for you. Do the work daily to learn and affirm the words for yourself, then allow my words and the words of others to confirm what you've learned about yourself.

Reflections

Chapter 5

You

ARE NOT ALONE

The world population one year before I wrote these words was 7,794,798,739 people. To be clear, that is a whole lot of people. It is incredible how we can be in a crowded world believing that we are all alone.

"I'm the only one who is screwed-up."

"I'm the only failure."

"Will a person on Earth love me or care for me from a pure place?"

"I am all alone."

I'm so *happy* that you picked up this book so I can tell you that I *love* you.

Have you ever found yourself believing that? Have you convinced yourself that of the 7,794,798,739 living and breathing today, you're the only one who doesn't have a life worth living? If you have, I'm so happy that you picked up this book so I can tell you that I love you. Even if we've never met, you were in my heart when I started writing. If the words speak to or resonate with you in any way, I want you to believe it is proof that you aren't by yourself.

Every lesson written in this book was written in part from a place of experience. I've cried too many tears, grown through too much brokenness, and healed from too many dark spaces in my life to let you think you're the only one who feels like you do. You aren't. I see you, and the only reason I see you is because you are the apple of God's eye.

I realize it can be controversial to talk about God, and some don't believe He exists. I quit running from my shadow, quit being afraid of my greatness, quit neglecting what I needed, and quit basing my esteem on the opinions of others. Today, I'm healthy enough to confidently stand on life as I understand it. For so long, I believed that no one could understand me. They were not present when life hurt the most. I put up a great front when I didn't feel the best. I desperately wanted people to know me, but at some point, I quit knowing myself. Life got much worse when I stopped thinking I was worth knowing.

There were nights I wondered how I could end it all, if anyone would miss me if I was gone. I felt about as low as life could feel. In the end, I'm not here to write this book because of fancy letters after my name. I am writing this because I was loved and empowered by something bigger than me, healed by something greater than me, and was made whole by a force that I can't quite fathom. In 2016, I felt hopeless. In 2017, I was counseling and spreading hope. My life changed in a hurry, in a way I can't take credit for. No meetings. No interventions. Only deliverance that could only come from something greater than me.

Your *shadow* behind you is the proof that there is a light in front of you to expose your *greatness* within

Now, I want to assure you, you are not alone. Whatever it is you want out of this life, whether it is growing that business, establishing your legacy on earth, building the marriage you've dreamed of, or anything else that it might be, I want you to know that I believe in you. I wasn't alone then and you aren't alone now. Some people in life have been praying you would call them. There are preachers and teachers, doctors and therapists waiting for you to walk into their office. There are business mentors and writing coaches who are waiting for what you're holding back. It doesn't have to be this way.

What if you are on this earth for such a time as this? (Esther 4:14). What if everything you've done and been through was all taking you to this place and this moment so that you could have your "ah-ha" moment'? Remember, the shadow is only dark behind you because of the light that sits ahead of you. Your future can be bright, but you need to stop trying to do this alone. It's not fair to you. It's equally not fair to the people you've been poisoning while they've tried to love you.

If you've been trying to walk with the weight of the world on your shoulders, stop. Quit. Jesus said, "Come to me, all of you who are weary and carry heavy burdens, and I will give you rest" (Matthew 11:28). You've been trying to do it alone and it is not working. You're tired.

You feel beat up. It's time that you surrender to a power that is greater than you and get the rest you need. Don't wait until tomorrow, tomorrow isn't promised.

Today is the gift you've been given. Close your eyes and let go of the pain you've been carrying for too long. Seriously, right now. It's ok to say that you're not ok and that it hurts like hell. Just don't stay in a living hell when heaven is waiting for you. Stop trying to be the strong one and be the one who is given strength by the One who is far stronger than you.

In a world of 7,794,798,739 people, you are neither a mistake nor are you alone. You're right where you need to be. Now is the time to learn who you truly are, so you can become what God is calling you to become. He declares, "Before I formed you in the womb I knew you before you were born I set you apart." You are not alone, you just were set apart for this season for a reason. It is time to do the work to begin to see yourself how He does. I can't wait to hear how it goes.

Reflections

Chapter 6

Save

THE DAY

After losing brothers in back-to-back years, I learned what a gift a day is. The fact that you've made it this far in life is a miracle in and of itself.

You made some poor choices?

Taken some unwise risks?

Had moments when you didn't appreciate or value life?

Life has not been perfect, but you are still here and still breathing. I want to challenge you to see the gift that you have in front of you. Scripture says "I have set before you life and death, blessings and curses. Now choose life" (Deuteronomy 30:19).

I pray this is the day you choose life. Love this day like a gift, because it is. Anything dragging you down, stealing your peace, or leaving you void of the quality of life you deserve has to be examined and challenged. Have you convinced yourself of the need for nouns that don't belong to you? There are people, places, and things that are not good for you , so you need to decide to choose life and quit the things and people who are killing you from the inside out.

I want you to know I am practicing what I preach. In the last few months, I've quit many situations that weren't serving me well. Sometimes when you quit something, it requires mourning afterward. Sometimes you need to grieve what you quit, but you still need to leave what you left behind. Leave with the lessons and the wisdom. Leave the negativity and the doubts behind.

Your shadow behind you is the proof that there is a light in front of you to expose your greatness within. You need to do the work for yourself to see what you are made of and how valuable you are. You aren't alone in this. You've been empowered by Power and loved by Love. If you are a believer, you have the Holy Spirit within you and Angels who surround you. If God is with you, who can stand against you? (Romans 8:31). It is time for you to embrace this gift God has given you and save the day.

Reflections

Afterword

Matthew 6:33-34

But seek first the kingdom of God and his righteousness, and all these things will be added to you. "Therefore do not be anxious about tomorrow, for tomorrow will be anxious for itself. Sufficient for the day is its own trouble."

I am aware that many books labeled "self-help" aim to empower you to find and "live your truth." That was honestly not my goal in writing Save the Day. Instead, it is my prayer that you are enlightened by the fact that Jesus is the way, the truth and the life (John 14:6). The direction, perception, and abundance that you are looking for all flow forth from Jesus. "Seek ye first the Kingdom of God and it's righteousness and all these things will be added to you." (Matthew 6:33-34 KJV). In other words, saving the day begins by worshipping and seeking intimacy with the God who created the day. Let your approach to healing flow forth from the Word of God and the Rhema word of the Holy Spirit (your inner hero). God will guide you and lead you into all things.

"So if the Son sets you free, you will be free indeed." (John 8:36).

If you have accepted Jesus as your Lord and savior, I believe you have been given true freedom. That being said, I meet men and women daily who have not started to walk in the freedom that God has given them. Guilt, shame, grief, remorse, and pain from their past have left them believing they are still in bondage. I wrote Save the Day to remind people that their actions are critically important. Jesus has made you free, but experiencing the fullness, freedom, and abundance that Jesus has promised us is a journey.

I wanted to take the time to share these thoughts because I know that writing about a topic like the one presented in this book can potentially lead to confusion about the principles I stand on. I felt as though the Holy Spirit was leading me to make it plain.

I believe God is faithful to finish what He started (Philippians 1:6), but the realization of His promises can require our participation.

Save the Day was not written to lead you to believe you can be or replace God. Instead, it is a wake up call that some of you have been waiting for God, but God is waiting for you. "So also faith by itself, if it does not have works, is dead." (James 2:20 ESV). Even after God performs miracles, signs, and wonders in our life, there is still an active role He wants us to play so that we fully realize His glory. Even the Disciples who walked with Jesus struggled with faith and obedience while they walked with him.

He said to his disciples, "Why are you so afraid? Do you still have no faith?" (John 4:40).

I'll draw your attention to the word "still." Even

after they had seen the works of Jesus in the flesh, they still had issues with their faith. They had to continue to walk with Him, to grow, learn, and mature in order to grow closer to Him and to Abba.

My prayer is that Save the Day serves as a reminder that you are important to God. As was the case with Jeremiah (Jeremiah 1:4-10), I believe He knew you before He formed you in your mother's womb. There is a plan for your life, but that plan requires your participation. God will supply the provision, protection, and peace, just make sure that you give Him your full participation, trust, and faith in return. Despite your rough past, you have been redeemed (Ephesians 1:7)! Behold, He is doing a new thing in you (Isaiah 43:19)!

Prayer of Salvation

If you have been reading this book and are wondering what you must do to be saved, I am so grateful for you! In the text, I state that "no one is coming to save you," but that is, in part, because the real Hero already has. Jesus paid a price for you and I. It is not too late for you to take Jesus as your Lord and savior right here and now. Just read these words and believe them in your heart:

Dear Lord Jesus, I know that I am a sinner, and I ask for Your forgiveness. I believe You died for my sins and rose from the dead. I turn from my sins and invite You to come into my heart and life. I want to trust and follow You as my Lord and Savior. In Your Name. Amen. Please reach out to me via my website and let me know that you spoke these words and took Jesus as your savior! We want to celebrate with you, pray for you, and encourage you as you move forward.

Please reach out to me via my website and let me know that you spoke these words and took Jesus as your savior! We want to celebrate with you, pray for you, and encourage you as you move forward.

Also, it would make a huge difference for me if you would go to **Amazon or Goodreads** and leave an honest review. There is nothing like honest feedback

For more information
www.mauricefmartin.com
@mauricefmartin

Want to sew a seed?
CashApp | $mauricefmartin
Venmo | @mauricefmartin

About The Author

Maurice F. Martin is an American entrepreneur and author. He is a premier inspirational speaker, chemical dependency counselor, and a certified life purpose coach. He is the co-host of Grace Factor Podcast. In 2020 Maurice released his Color Blind video to national acclaim. It was featured on the YouTube Original production Bear Witness Take Action and has been seen by over 4 million people. Maurice is a man of many talents. He is an award-winning vocalist and songwriter who has had his work licensed to VH-1, MTV, the Discovery Network, E!, and ABC. He is currently focusing attention on his second novel, Your But Is Too Big. Maurice lives in Akron, Ohio with his wife and their two children.

Made in the USA
Middletown, DE
20 October 2022

13107241R00043